THE SUPREME COURT

A TRUE BOOK

by

Patricia Ryon Quiri

Children's Press®
A Division of Grolier Publishing

New York London Hong Kong Sydney
Danbury, Connecticut

Reading Consultant
Linda Cornwell
Learning Resource Consultant
Indiana Department
of Education

Author's Dedication:
For all the schoolchildren
I have taught
Be the best you can be.
With Love, Mrs. Quiri.

The official seal of the
U.S. Supreme Court

Visit Children's Press on the Internet at:
http://publishing.grolier.com

Library of Congress Cataloging-in-Publication Data

Quiri, Patricia Ryon.
   The Supreme Court / by Patricia Ryon Quiri.
      p.   cm. — (A true book)
   Includes bibliographical references and index.
   Summary: A history and description of the Supreme Court of the
United States, explaining its origins in the Constitutional Convention, its
early history, and some landmark cases.
   ISBN 0-516-20679-6 (lib. bdg.)   0-516-26441-9 (pbk.)
   1. United States. Supreme Court—History—Juvenile literature.[1.
United States. Supreme Court—History.] I. Title. II. Series.
KF8742.Z9Q57   1998   97-48950
347.73'26—dc21   CIP
                                                              AC

Contents

The Constitutional Convention in Philadelphia

Strengthening the Federal Government

In May 1787, fifty-five Americans met at the State House in Philadelphia. The meeting took place only four years after the United States won its independence from Britain. At the time, the federal, or national, government of the United States was still very weak. Its laws could not be enforced throughout the land. The purpose of the meeting was to make a plan for a stronger federal government.

Many of the delegates who came to the meeting were famous. They included George Washington, who led the Americans to victory against the British and became the first president of the United States. They also included James

Madison, who became the fourth president of the United States, and Alexander Hamilton, who believed in a strong federal government.

For four long, hot months, the delegates made a plan for the new government. During this time, they created the document known as the Constitution. The Constitution spelled out the powers of the federal government. It stated that the federal government

The Constitution of
the United States

would be made up of three
branches. The executive
branch would be headed by a

president, who would make sure that the laws of the country were obeyed. The legislative branch, called Congress, would make the laws. Finally, the judicial branch would see that the laws of the country were understood.

The three branches of government served as checks and balances on one another. In other words, none of the three had more power than the other.

The Judicial Branch

After the Constitution was written, the leaders of the nation set up the judicial branch. This branch of government is made up of federal judges, also called justices. The justices help people understand the laws of the United States. The judicial branch is the home of the Supreme Court of the United States, the highest court in the land. This court makes legal decisions by following the rules laid down by the Constitution. It also examines decisions made by less important courts.

The Constitution did not state how many Supreme Court justices there should be. In 1789, there were six. Between the years 1863

The first justices of the Supreme Court (from left to right): John Jay (Chief Justice), James Tredell, John Blair, William Cushing, James Wilson, and John Rutledge

and 1866, there were ten. However, from 1869 on, there have been nine justices. One

of these serves as the head,
or chief, justice.

The president of the
United States chooses each
justice. Then the candidate

The Senate did not approve of President Reagan's appointment of Robert Bork as a Surpeme Court justice.

must be approved by the Senate, which is part of the legislative branch. Sometimes the Senate does not approve a president's choice. For example, in 1987, the Senate did not approve the appointment of Robert Bork by President Reagan.

Until recently, all the justices were white men. However, in 1967, the Court's first African-American justice, Thurgood Marshall, was appointed. In

Thurgood Marshall (left), the first African-American Supreme Court justice, and Sandra Day O'Connor (right), the first woman to serve on the Supreme Court

1981, the first woman justice, Sandra Day O'Connor, joined the Supreme Court.

Each justice serves the Court for the rest of the person's life, or until he or she retires. If a Supreme Court justice does not do the job right, the Senate can impeach that person, which means they can try to remove the person from the Court. However, this has never happened to any justice on the Supreme Court.

What the Supreme Court Does

The Supreme Court, like any other court of law, helps to settle arguments between people. It handles cases that involve our understanding of the Constitution. When the Supreme Court makes a decision on a case, that decision

The Supreme Court hears a case in the early 1900s.

is final, and it becomes a model for similar future cases.

Cases that go to the Supreme Court are named for the people involved. If two people have an argument that is judged by the Supreme Court, the case is named after them. Suppose Mr. Smith sues Mr. Green. The Supreme Court would call this case *Smith v. Green.*

The *v* stands for the word *versus*, which means *against*. Now let's say that Mr. Brown is suing the government. Then the case would be called *Brown v. United States.*

The nine justices listen to cases and then vote. Each justice has only one vote, and the majority rules. A majority vote could be a 9–0 vote. It could be 8–1. Or it could be a close vote: 5–4.

Chief Justice John Marshall

John Marshall was the fourth chief justice of the Supreme Court. Many people think he was the best chief justice the country ever had. He served from 1801 to 1835 and helped make the Supreme Court strong and respected.

Chief Justice John Marshall

James Madison (left) and William Marbury

John Marshall was chief justice when a case called *Marbury v. Madison* came to the Supreme Court. The year was 1803. William Marbury was a politician, and James

Madison was secretary of state under President Thomas Jefferson. (Madison would later become the fourth president of the United States.) In this case, the Supreme Court struck down an act of Congress that went against the Constitution. *Marbury v. Madison* was one of the most important cases in U.S. history. It gave the Supreme Court more power to interpret the laws of the U.S. Constitution.

The Supreme Court After Marshall

During the Civil War (1861–1865), the southern states tried to leave the United States and form a separate country. But the South was defeated, and the southern states remained part of the United States. When the war was over, many cases

before the Supreme Court con-
cerned states' rights.

In a case called *Texas v. White*
(1868), the Court ruled that even
if a state had rebelled against
the United States, it still
remained a state. Almost 30
years later, in 1895, the Court
made decisions about how the
federal government could collect
income tax from states. This rul-
ing led to a new amendment to
the Constitution. An amendment
is a change to a legal document.

Close-Up of a Case:

White v. Texas, 1868

The Lone Star flag of the Republic of Texas

Can a state declare itself independent of the Union? Texas claimed to be independent two times in its history. In 1836, Texas rebelled from Mexico and became the Republic of Texas. During the Civil War, Texas and other southern states broke away from the United States.

After the Civil War, the Supreme Court decided in *Texas v. White* that it was illegal for a state to leave the Union. The Court said that Texas had always been a state, whether or not it had rebelled.

Signers of the Ordinance of Secession, which declared Texas independent of the United States

Money used in Texas and other southern states after they left the Union

The Supreme Court in Recent Times

In the 1950s and 1960s, the Supreme Court made important decisions about civil rights. Up until that time, segregation was legal in some parts of the South. Segregation is the practice of separating blacks and whites in schools, hospitals,

Earl Warren, chief justice during the 1950s and 1960s

and other public facilities. In a case called *Brown v. Board of Education of Topeka* (1954),

A few years after *Brown v. Board of Education*, some African-American students in the South still needed military guards to get safely to school.

the Supreme Court ruled that segregation was against the Constitution. The Court said that blacks should be able to go to the same schools as whites.

During the same period, the Court made a decision about the rights of people who are arrested. In a case called *Miranda v. Arizona* (1966), the

Ernesto Miranda (right), whose arrest led to *Miranda v. Arizona* in 1966

court ruled that anyone who is accused of a crime must be told of his or her right to remain silent and his or her right to have a lawyer present.

In the 1980s, the Court made stricter rules for workers who sued employers because they thought their employer had discriminated against them. A person who discriminates treats people unfairly because of their race, sex, religion, or other factors. The

Court also ruled that murderers as young as sixteen could be put to death.

William H. Rehnquist, who was appointed chief justice of the Supreme Court in 1986

The Supreme Court Today

The Supreme Court building is located in Washington, D.C. It stands near the Capitol, where Congress meets.

The Supreme Court building has many different rooms. These include the courtroom and several libraries as well as meeting rooms and offices.

The Supreme Court building, Washington, D.C.

The Supreme Court follows many old traditions. For example, quill pens—pens made of feathers—are still used in the Court. A seamstress is hired to sew and mend the robes worn by the justices.

The Supreme Court hears about two hundred cases from October until June. Court begins at 10:00 A.M. and goes on until noon. Then it starts again at 1:00 P.M. and goes on until 3:00 P.M. The justices listen

A law clerk doing research in a law library

to the cases and then meet with one another to discuss them. Their law clerks go to the libraries to look for information that will be helpful.

The Supreme Court plays an important role in the lives of all Americans. The decisions the justices make affect everyone. They make sure the Constitution is understood and followed and help protect the rights of all the citizens of the United States.

The justices of the Supreme Court. Seated, front row: Antonin Scalia, John Paul Stevens, William H. Rehnquist, Sandra Day O'Connor, and Anthony Kennedy. Standing, back row: Ruth Bader Ginsburg, David Souter, Clarence Thomas, and Stephen Breyer.

Inside the Supreme Court

The Supreme Court is more than just a courtroom. Its many rooms have everything needed to study, discuss, and rule on cases that come before it.

◀ The opposite page shows the courtroom of the Supreme Court. No photos can be taken while the Court is in session.

The Supreme Court Library ▼

▲ The chambers (office) of Associate Justice Sandra Day O'Connor

To Find Out More

Here are some additional resources to help you learn more about the Supreme Court:

 **Books**

Friedman, Leon. **The Supreme Court.** Chelsea House Publishers, 1987.

Morris, Richard. **The Constitution.** Lerner Publications Company, 1985.

Peterson, Helen. **The Supreme Court in America's Story.** Garrard Publishing, 1976.

Quiri, Patricia Ryon. **The Constitution.** Children's Press, 1998.

Stein, Conrad. **The Story of the Powers of the Supreme Court.** Children's Press, 1989.

💡 Organizations and Online Sites

Constitutional Rights Foundation
601 S. Kingsley Drive
Los Angeles, CA 90005

Helps young people understand the values of the Constitution.

National Archives
700 Pennsylvania Ave. NW
Washington, DC 20408

The original document of the Constitution is on display.

Justices of the Supreme Court
http://supct.law.cornell.edu/ supct/justices/fullcourt.html

Pictures and biographies of all the justices of the Supreme Court.

Time for Kids
http://www.pathfinder.com/ @@C5kkv6BlgglAQGgs/TF K/index.html

Keep informed about politics with this online version of *Time* magazine for young people.

Uncle Sam for Kids
www.win.org/library/mtls/ govdocs/kids.htm

A wide range of links about government and politics.

Important Words

amendment a change in a legal document

Capitol building where members of Congress meet

Congress lawmaking body of the U.S. government

Constitution written laws of the U.S. government

discriminate treat unfairly

executive presidential; branch of government that makes sure laws are obeyed

impeach to try to remove someone from office

judicial belonging to a branch of government that makes sure laws are understood

legislative lawmaking

segregation separation of the races

versus against

Index

Meet the Author

Patricia Ryon Quiri lives in Palm Harbor, Florida, with her husband Bob and three sons. Ms. Quiri graduated from Alfred University in upstate New York and has a B.A. in elementary education. She currently teaches second grade in the Pinellas County School system. Other books by Ms. Quiri include *The Presidency*, *The Declaration of Independence*, *The Constitution*, and *The Bill of Rights*. Ms. Quiri has also written a five-book series on American landmarks and symbols and several books for Franklin Watts.